# Flannelboard Stories
# for
# Infants and Toddlers

## Ann Carlson
## and
## Mary Carlson, Illustrator

AMERICAN LIBRARY ASSOCIATION
Chicago and London
1999

Cover design by Mary Carlson

Text design and composition by Ann Carlson using Chantilly (a.k.a. Gill Sans) and MS Comic Sans

The paper used in this publication meets the minimum requirements of American National Standard for Information Sciences—Permanence of Paper for Printed Library Materials, ANSI Z39.48-1992. ∞

**Library of Congress Cataloging-in-Publication Data**

Carlson, Ann D., 1952–
    Flannelboard stories for infants and toddlers / Ann Carlson :
illustrated by Mary Carlson.
      p.   cm.
    ISBN 0-8389-0759-8
    1. Flannel boards.  2. Storytelling.  3. Children's stories, American.
4. Toddlers—Recreation.  5. Infants—Recreation.  I. Carlson, Mary,
1951– .  II. Title.
LB1043.62.C37  1999
371.33'5—dc21                      98-54724

Printed in the United States of America.

03  02  01  00  99      5 4 3 2 1

For Ateş and Jim

# Contents

# Preface

This book is a collection of easy-to-make, high quality flannelboard stories that are appropriate for infants and toddlers — children between 12 and 30 months of age. We have designed it to be used by librarians, early childhood teachers, and other adults who work with groups of these young children.

The book contains step-by-step instructions on (1) how to make a flannelboard, (2) how to make flannelboard pieces for the stories and verses, and (3) how to store flannelboard stories. The body of the book consists of uncomplicated full-size patterns for 33 stories and verses. The index offers object and theme subject headings for effective access to the stories and pattern pieces.

We see three reasons you will find this book worthwhile:

1.  **Convenience and Cost-Effectiveness**
    Preparing flannelboard stories from picture books and magazines can be very expensive in terms of staff time, considering the effort of locating illustrations and converting them to flannelboard format.

2.  **Developmental Appropriateness**
    It is very important to select flannelboard stories that are developmentally appropriate for the intended audience. However, the scarcity of resources for infants and toddlers means having to frequently make do with materials that are more suitable for older children.

The flannelboard stories in this book were designed especially to appeal to the one- and two-year-old, and they have been used in storytimes with good results.

3. **No Copyright Violation**

   We are all concerned about the issue of copyright violation. Unless a work is in the public domain, it is a violation of copyright law to adapt its illustrations or text for a flannelboard story and present it as your own. We grant individual librarians and teachers permission to duplicate the patterns in this book for non-commercial use with children. You do not need to be concerned with copyright violation.

We hope you will find the material in this book clear, practical, and aesthetically pleasing. Even more importantly, we hope that the children who attend your storytimes enjoy and benefit from the stories and illustrations we offer. We wish you successful storytimes with your infants and toddlers!

# Introduction
# and
# Instructions to the User

The widespread use of flannelboards in storytimes is a relatively recent development. Articles extolling the virtues of flannelboards began appearing in the education literature in the mid-1950s. An excellent example is Alpha Boggs and Ruth Schofield's "A Piece of Flannel and a Bit of Imagination" in the September 1956 issue of *National Elementary Principal*. The authors, who were consultants for the St. Louis, Missouri, Public Schools, point out that they did not come up with the idea: "Rather, they have seen so many fine and varied uses of this instructional aid during their supervisory visits, that they have tried only to gather the representative ones together and pass them along to others."[1]

Boggs and Schofield suggested that the flannelboard is valuable because: (1) it is portable; (2) it has a magic quality that appeals to children; (3) it permits manipulation, a decided attraction to children; (4) it re-emphasizes book presentation but in a slightly different form; and (5) it is inexpensive.[2] These reasons still hold today.

*Storytelling with the Flannel Board* by Paul S. Anderson, published in 1963, appears to have been the first commercial book with patterns for flannelboard stories. In it the author states that his training as a soldier in World War II introduced him to the flannelboard:

> As a part of the training program in the last war, flannelgraph was used to illustrate troop movements, traffic control problems

and map reading in much the same manner as a sand table might be used. The flannel board has the advantage of being upright so that a class can watch it in the same way that they would use a blackboard.[3]

It seems plausible that teachers who served in the war incorporated the flannelboard into their teaching techniques after the war and that other teachers and librarians then adopted the technique for storytimes.

No matter what its genesis, the flannelboard has been and still is a vital part of many library and classroom storytimes. Today, with an increasing number of libraries and child care facilities in day care centers, hospitals, and schools offering storytimes for infants and toddlers, flannelboard stories should be even more widely used.

The flannelboard story has characteristics particularly suited to an audience of infants and toddlers: It displays images larger and less cluttered than those in most picture books; it renders visual clues to the next verse in a song or refrain in a poem; it exposes children to the sequencing conventions of the written page; and it provides variety by offering an alternative format.

The flannelboard story has clear benefits for the librarian or educator working with an audience of infants and toddlers as well: It encourages participation of parents and caregivers; it adds variety to storytimes; and, it offers adaptability in terms of image selection, image production, and style of presentation as described below.

## The Use of Text

You will notice that the patterns in this book include the written name of the pictured object, the text from the poem or nursery rhyme, or the title of the story. We have designed the patterns so that you can trace or copy the text onto the pieces. (The occasional instruction on patterns in small print is not intended to be traced or copied onto the piece.) The text may help children understand that the black squiggles on the piece stand for words that the adults are saying. The text can also act as a prompt to the adults in the audience so that they all call out the same words. It has been our experience that when a group of parents or caregivers of infants and toddlers see the illustration of a cat, for example, some will say "cat" and others "kitty."

# Adaptability of Flannelboard Stories

When it comes to storytimes for infants and toddlers, adaptability is paramount. Depending on your audience, you can adapt the stories and patterns in this book in three different ways:

1.  **Selection of patterns**
    As you look through the stories, consider the age range of your audience. If it is primarily made up of 12- to 18-month-olds, choose one of the simpler stories that centers around object identification, such as "Animals," and present the images of just a few more common animals. Since young children benefit from repetition, you can present additional animals in subsequent storytimes and as the children mature. This way you will repeat some animals while introducing new ones.

2.  **Production of pattern pieces**
    You can produce pieces suitable for different stories or presentations by varying the colors of objects, the skin tones of people, and the sizes of images.

3.  **Placement of pieces on the board**
    Pieces can be presented on the flannelboard in several different ways. Some librarians and teachers enjoy placing and keeping all the pieces on the board as they tell the story. Others prefer to place each piece on the board as it is used and then remove it before going on. In large part, you will do what feels best for you. However, when dealing with infants and young toddlers, we use the "slow solo piece" method: Sitting to one side of the board, we place one piece on the center of the board, read the text, and talk about the object as appropriate; we then remove the piece before placing the succeeding piece on the board. This style allows the young children time to focus their attention on one piece.

In subsequent storytimes and as the children grow, you may want to consider accumulating the pieces on the flannelboard while you tell the story. Start by placing the first piece in the upper left-hand corner of the board. Then, as shown in the illustration, place pieces in rows across the board, proceeding

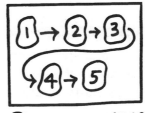

Piece sequence

from left to right and top to bottom, thereby introducing the children to the conventions of reading a page.

## How to Make a Flannelboard and Pieces

### Making a Flannelboard

You can purchase a flannelboard from various commercial supply companies that cater to libraries, schools, and businesses. You can also make one yourself by following the instructions in this section.

1. Cut a 2-by-3-foot rectangle out of thin plywood or rugged corrugated board. Appliance containers, such as those used for refrigerators and washing machines, are excellent since the corrugated board is much thicker than that found in the typical corrugated box.

2. Cut a piece of solid color flannel, felt, or acrylic fleece 6 to 8 inches wider and longer than the board. We suggest a dark color for your first board.

3. Tightly stretch the fabric over the board and fasten it to the back of the board with duct tape, staples, tacks, or glue. If you choose to use glue, make sure not to glue the flannel to the front of the board since it will keep the pattern pieces from sticking to the flannel.

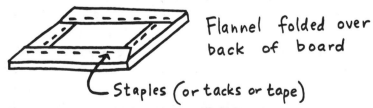

Depending on the stories you tell and how you tell them, you may need flannelboards of various sizes. Some stories offered here are best told one piece at a time, while others are better told by accumulating the pieces on the board as the story progresses. Consider having on hand a few boards of various sizes and colors.

In time, if you find that your flannelboard pieces will no longer stick to the board, try brushing the flannel with a lint-removing brush. If that does not work, take the fabric off and wash it or replace it with a fresh piece. If you wash the flannel, do not use fabric softener in the washer or dryer since static cling is actually desirable.

A flannelboard should be propped on an easel. Easels are available through commercial supply companies for libraries, schools, and businesses, as well as at many office supply stores. A sturdy metal one with telescoping legs is a wise investment. Telescoping legs allow you to slide the legs to a height that is right for your group, especially if adults are sitting on the floor with their young children.

If you need a more portable flannelboard, you can create a folding one out of an artist's large portfolio carrier. Portfolios may be obtained through arts and crafts catalogs and art supply stores. Choose a sturdy one that will hold its shape.

Flannel board on easel

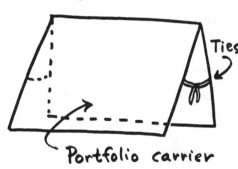

Ties

Portfolio carrier

Cover the portfolio with fabric so that the inside surface of one or both flaps constitutes a flannelboard. To use the portfolio, open it and bend it back over its spine to expose the inner surfaces. A portfolio that has fabric ties on the sides, as many do, will provide you with a ready means to tie the flaps together to keep it from collapsing. Otherwise, you will need to fashion your own ties.

Covering the flap(s) of the portfolio with fabric presents a bit more of a challenge than a plain board. You may have to cut the fabric in a more complex shape and experiment with different fasteners. Keep in mind that you can cover both flaps, which will give you two flannelboards, each one possibly a different color.

# Making Pieces for the Flannelboard Stories

We provide instructions for two methods of making pattern pieces: the tracing method and the copying machine method. Both have benefits and drawbacks.

## The Tracing Method

1. Buy a yard or so of white medium-to-heavy-weight Pellon Sew-In Interfacing at a fabric shop. Be sure to purchase the nonfusible type; do *not* buy the iron-on type.

2. Cut rectangles out of the inter-facing (around 8½" by 11" ex-cept for the patterns in "Getting Dressed" and "Where Is Your Bellybutton?"), one for each pat-tern page, including the story's title page.

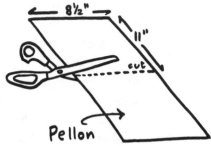

3. Place the interfacing rectangle over the pattern in the book and trace the outline of the pattern in pencil on the fabric.

4. Remove the outlined piece from the book and place it on a flat working surface. Go over the pencil tracing with a black felt-tip marker. We have designed these patterns with a fine-point perma-nent marker in mind. It is best to buy a good quality permanent

black marker to use exclusively for making your flannelboard pieces. If you use a washable marker, moisture from your hands may cause the ink to bleed. In addition, you will have the option of washing and ironing the pieces when they become dirty if you use permanent markers.

5.  Let the ink from the black marker dry thoroughly before you color the piece. It is best to use light colors for large areas within the outlines. Darker colors are difficult to apply uniformly to large areas, and pen strokes tend to remain visible. Once again, use good quality permanent markers. Sanford Sharpie fine-point markers are available in seven basic colors in addition to black. Prismacolor Double Nib markers are available in 144 colors, but at roughly twice the cost of the others.

    When you color a character or an object that runs through a story, take care to use the same color throughout. For example, color the sipping cup the same yellow throughout the "Sipping Cup."

6.  You may leave the rectangle piece as is or trim around the edge of the pattern to create a border, producing round-edged irregular shapes. However, do not cut right on the outline of the figure itself; otherwise, the edges of the pattern will look indistinct when placed on a flannelboard. Leave white space around the edges to create what we call a "puddle page."

Puddle cutting

There are advantages to the tracing method: The pieces will easily adhere to the flannelboard without having another material glued to their backs; they can be laundered if you have used permanent markers; and they are a bit easier to store. The obvious disadvantage is that it takes time to trace, outline, and color the pieces, which some people find tedious. Some do enjoy it, however, and feel a sense of pride in creating the pieces for the story.

## The Copying Machine Method

1.  Copy the patterns onto card-stock paper, using a copying machine. Any smooth white or light pastel paper that readily accepts color will work fine as long as you use the same color card stock throughout each story.

2.  Color the pieces. You can use ink markers, watercolors, tempera paints, and crayons to color the pieces. Depending upon the quality of your copying machine, you may want to go over the outlines with a black marker. Darker outlines tend to add depth to the appearance of a piece.

3.  For longer lasting pieces, laminate them or cover them with clear contact paper.

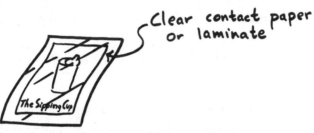

4.  If you laminate the pieces, trim the plastic to the edge of the paper. You may want to trim the pieces further as described earlier under the tracing method.

Trimming the plastic

5.  Glue felt or sandpaper or stick adhesive-backed Velcro tape to the back of each piece. You don't need to cover the entire back, but do cut the material to the general shape of the piece.

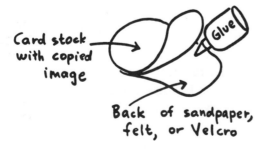

The primary advantage of this method is that it is faster than the tracing method, especially if the card stock and other materials are readily available. You can also enlarge or reduce the size of the image if the copying machine has that function. The obvious disadvantage is that you need to have access to a copying machine, heavy card-stock paper, and a laminator if contact paper is not used. Clear contact paper can be difficult to handle, and gluing the felt or sandpaper to the backs of the pieces can be messy.

## Storage of Flannelboard Stories

Storage methods for the story pieces are important. We offer the following suggestions.

- Keep each story in its own file folder. Store the pieces in a manila envelope large enough to accommodate them without bending.

- Separate the pieces with sheets of blank white paper. Some markers, especially black permanent ones, tend to bleed over time, and sandpaper can damage the finish on adjacent pieces.

- Take care that the corners of pieces are not bent and that they are packed flat. Creased pieces are distracting and hard to manipulate.

- Label the story file folder and the envelopes with the name of the story and, if appropriate, the names of individual pattern pieces. For example, on the "Let's Play" story file folder, list the names of the objects, such as blocks, keys, jack-in-the-box, and so on. You will then be able to locate a particular illustration if needed for another use. For example, you could use the jack-in-the-box piece from "Let's Play" for doing "Jack-in-the-box, he sits so still. Will he come out? Yes he will!"

- Arrange the story file folders so that you can locate them easily. We store stories with pieces larger than 8½" by 11" flat on a shelf with pieces of tagboard between them. For stories that will fit in 8½"-by-11" envelopes we use hanging files.

Hanging files

# Notes

1. Alpha Boggs and Ruth Schofield, "A Piece of Flannel and a Bit of Imagination," *National Elementary Principal* 35 (Sept. 1956): 237.
2. Ibid., 241.
3. Paul S. Anderson, *Storytelling with the Flannel Board* (Minneapolis: Denison, 1963), 7.

# Flannelboard Patterns

## Stories

# Can You Do This?

Clap your hands.

Stomp your feet.

Sway your body to the beat.

Open your fingers.

Point to your nose.

Put your arms in the air.

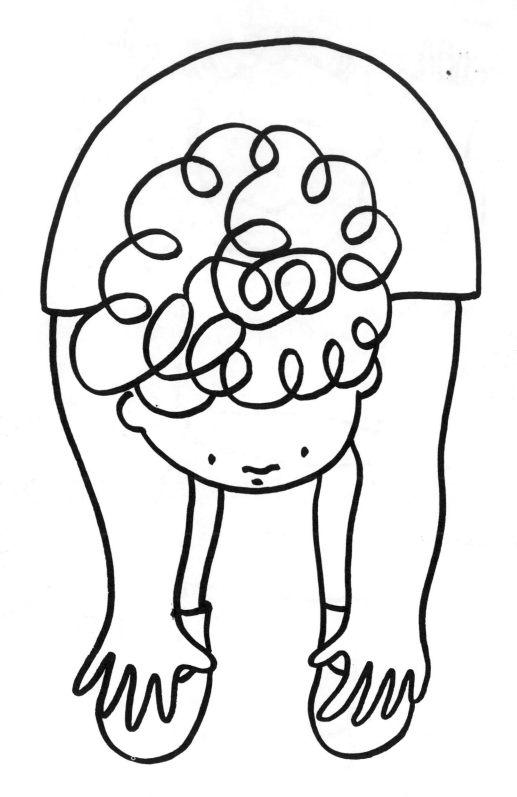

Now touch your toes.

# Pretend to Be

Can you guess what the child is pretending to be?

Can you pretend to be it?

a bird

an airplane

a tree

an elephant

# Look at Me

Yip, yow, yee,
Yip, yow, yee,

Stomp, stomp, stomp,

And look at me!

# Animals

You may want to talk about animal sounds; you may want to color the animals and talk about their colors. For example, when presenting the duck you may want to say, "Here's the duck. It is a white duck. The duck says 'quack, quack.' Can you make a sound like a duck?" Other questions about how the animal moves, what it eats, where it sleeps, and so forth are fun to ask older toddlers.

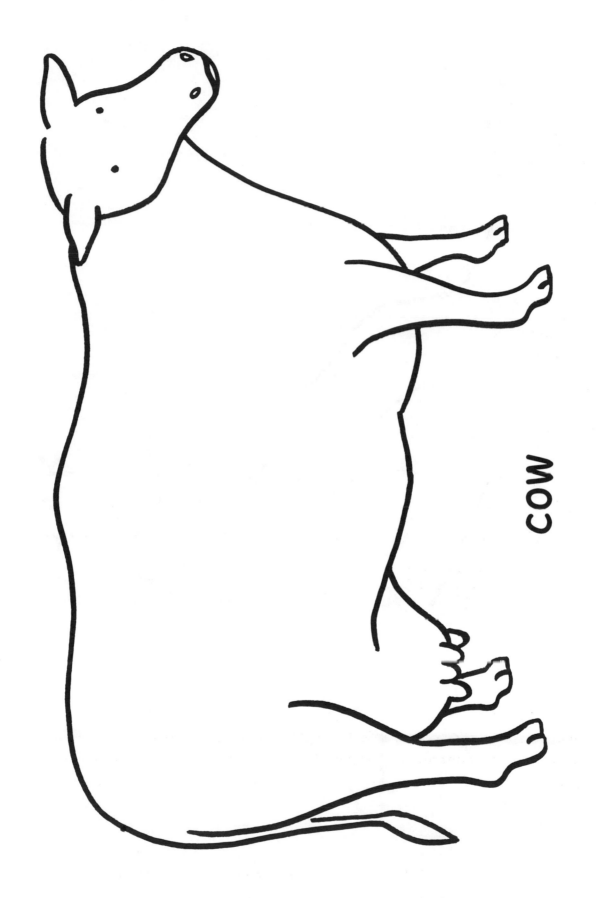

COW

31

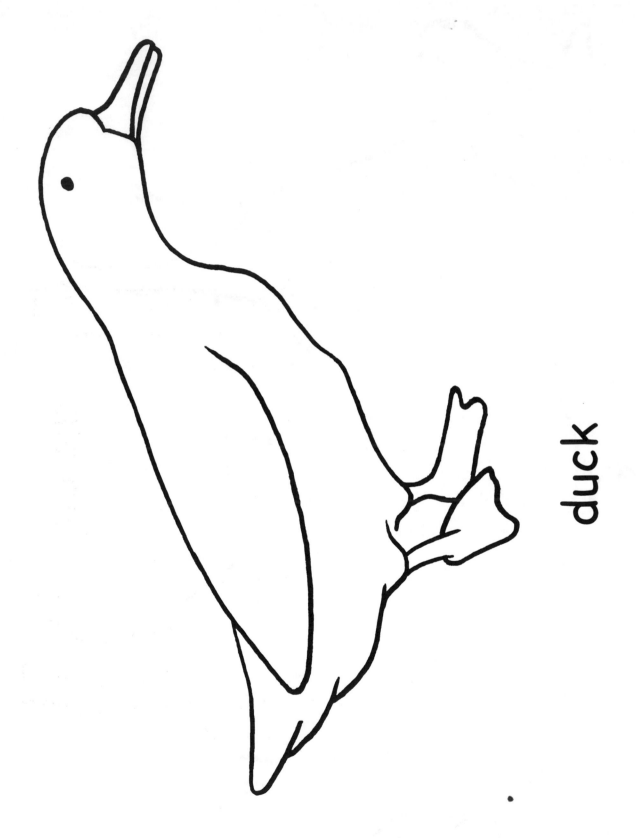

duck

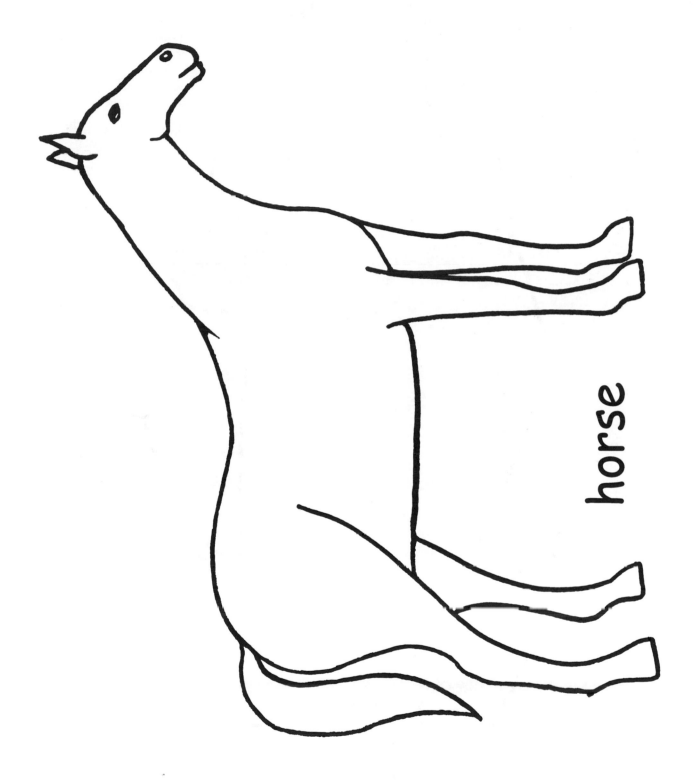

horse

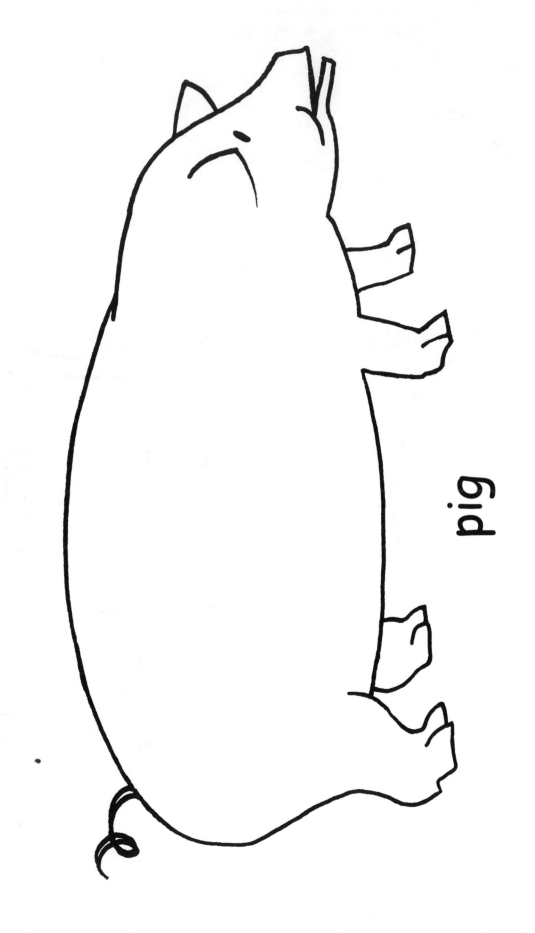

pig

34

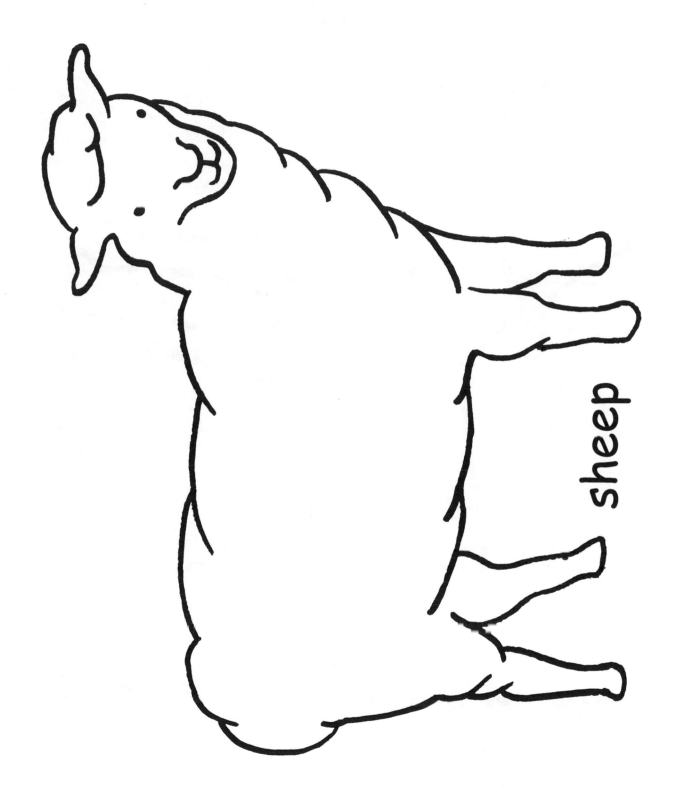

sheep

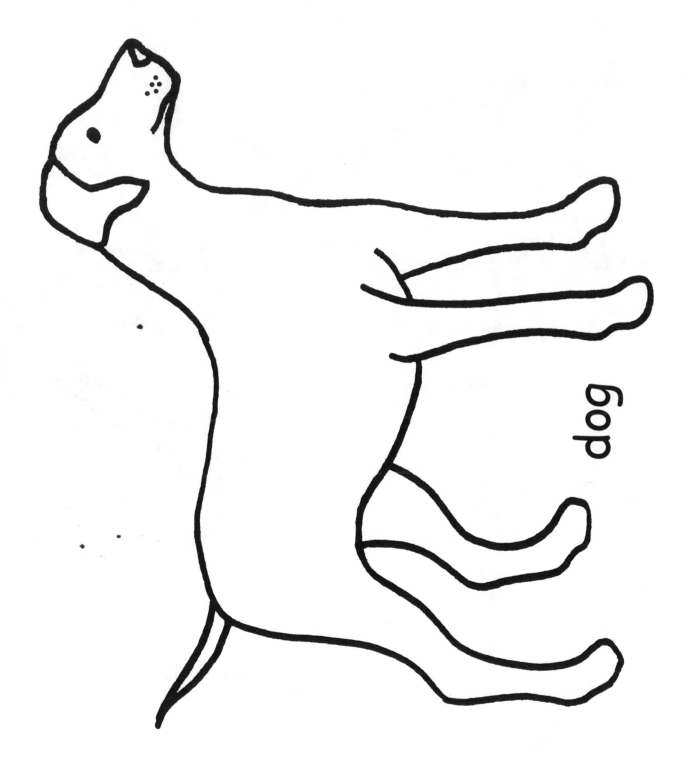

dog

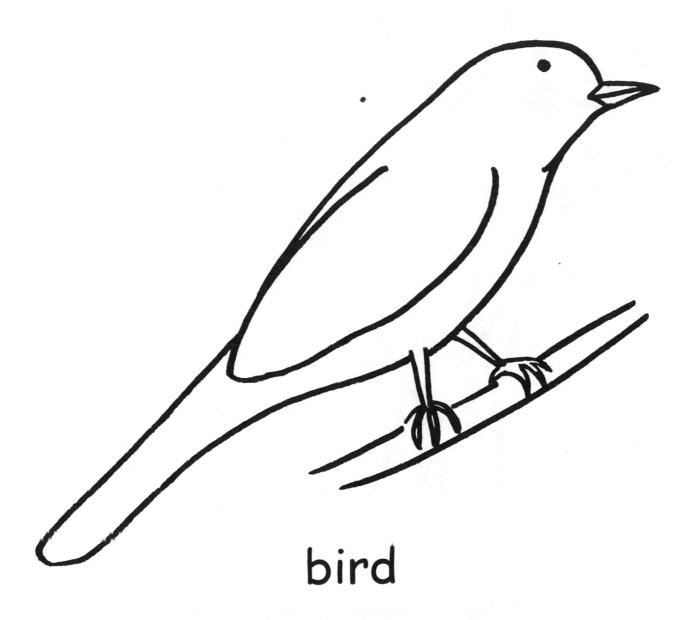

bird

cat

turkey

rooster

All together now!

# What Is This Baby Doing?

This baby is falling down.

... drinking from a bottle

... beating a drum

... drawing a picture

... rolling a ball

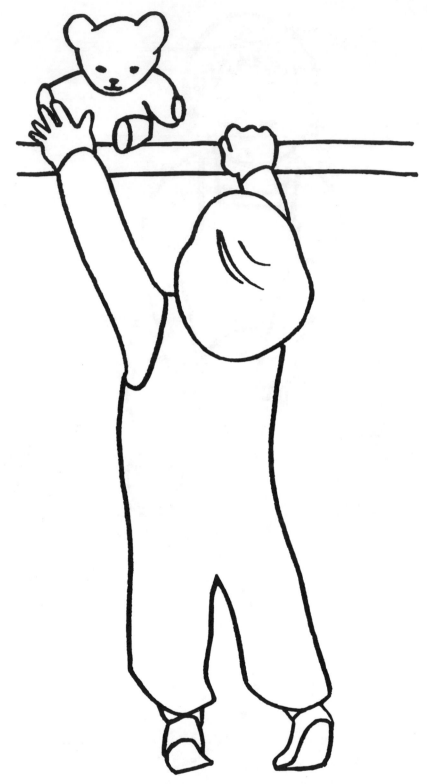

... reaching for a teddy bear

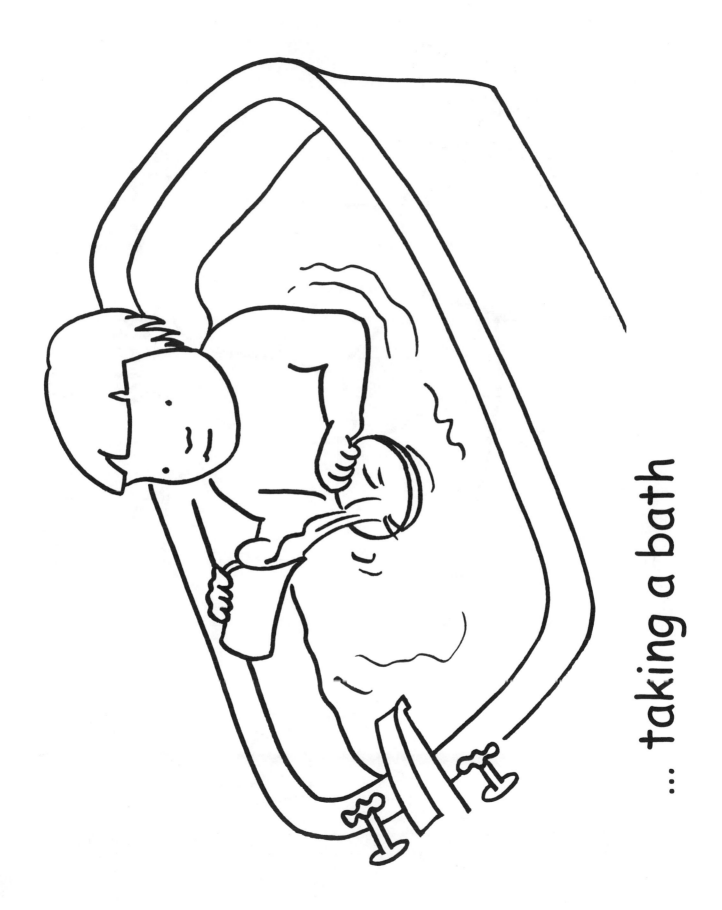

... taking a bath

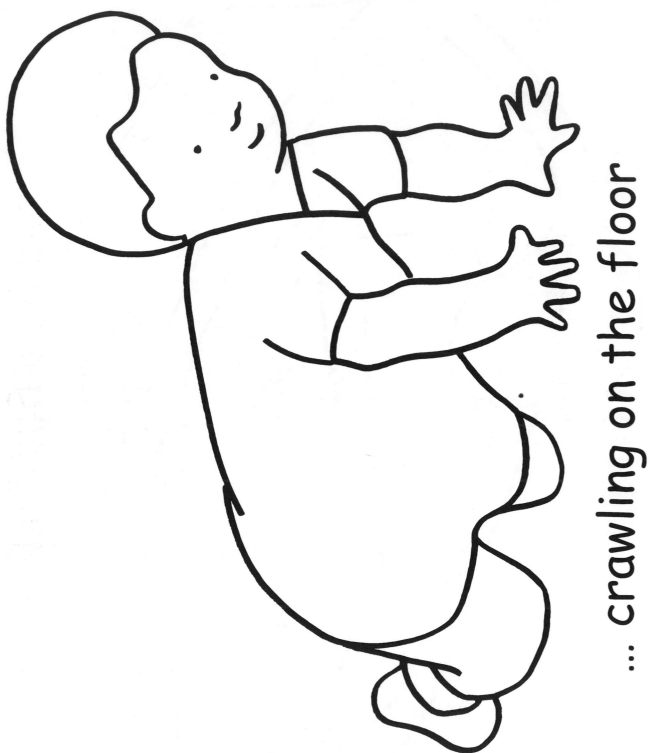

... crawling on the floor

... hugging a friend

... waving bye-bye

# Getting Dressed

This activity requires you to construct a large figure by combining the patterns on the following two pages. Unlike other pattern pieces, the figure and its clothing should be cut out close to the outlines so that the clothing makes contact with the flannelboard and sticks to it.

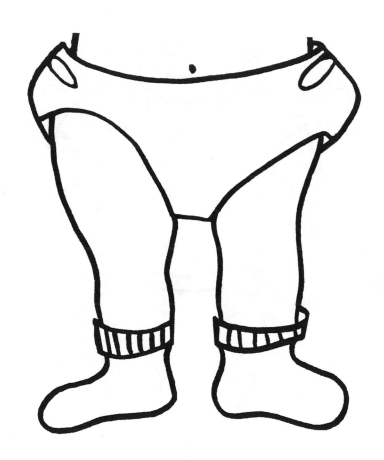

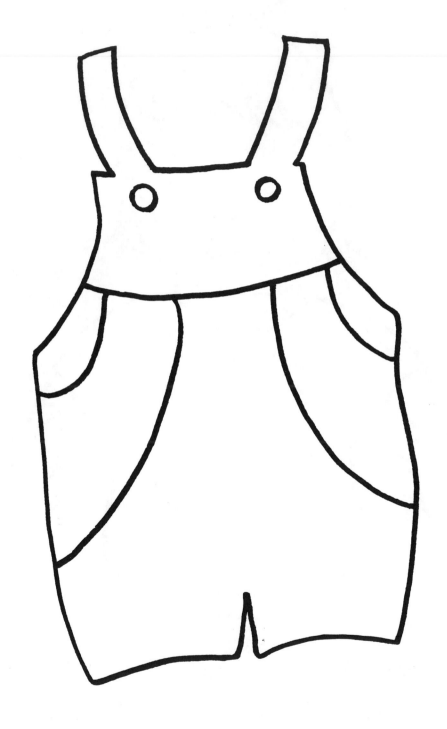

# What Is This Baby Feeling?

Look at the faces and see if you can tell.

What makes you feel the same way as the baby?

happy

sad

surprised

# My Favorite Foods

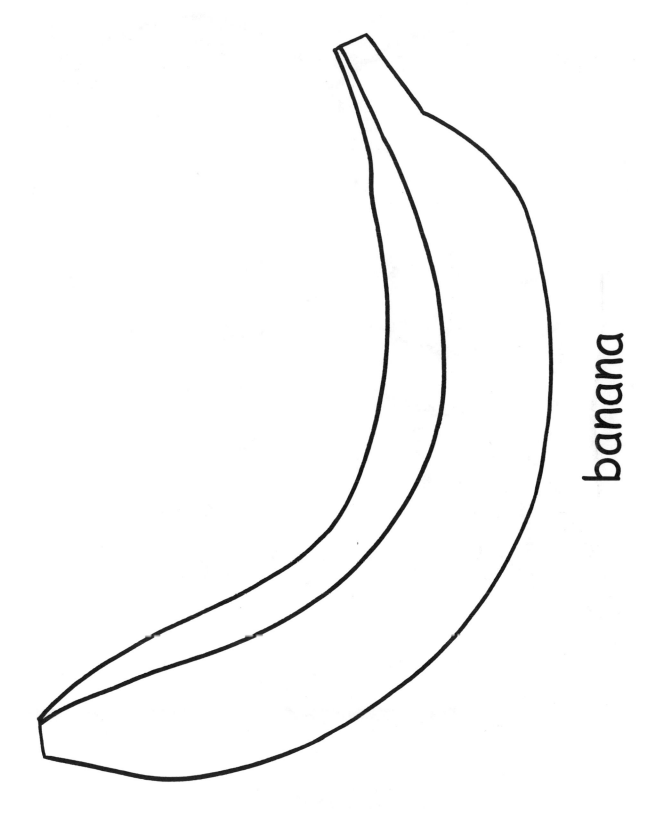

banana

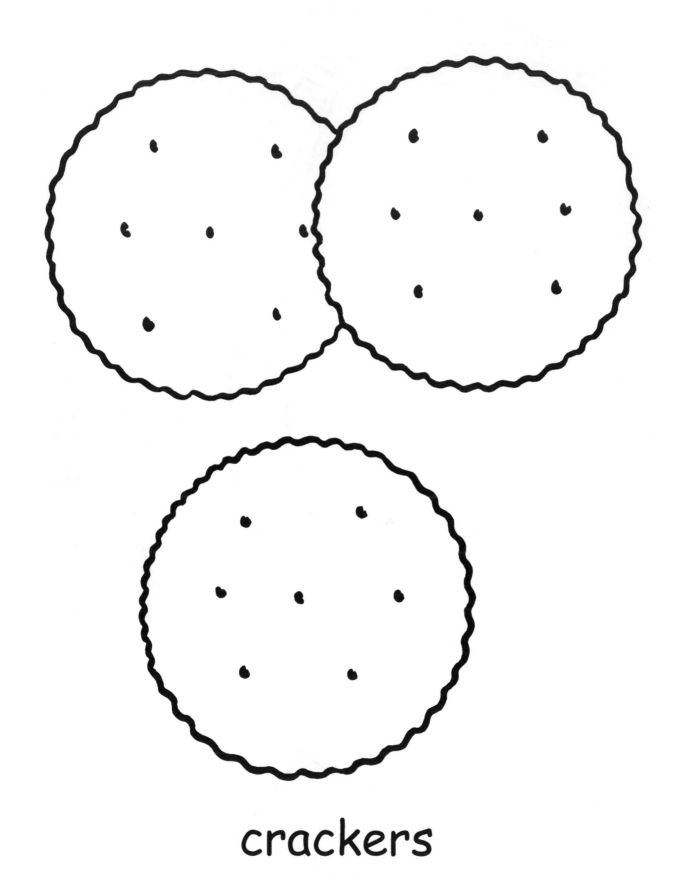

crackers

ice cream cone

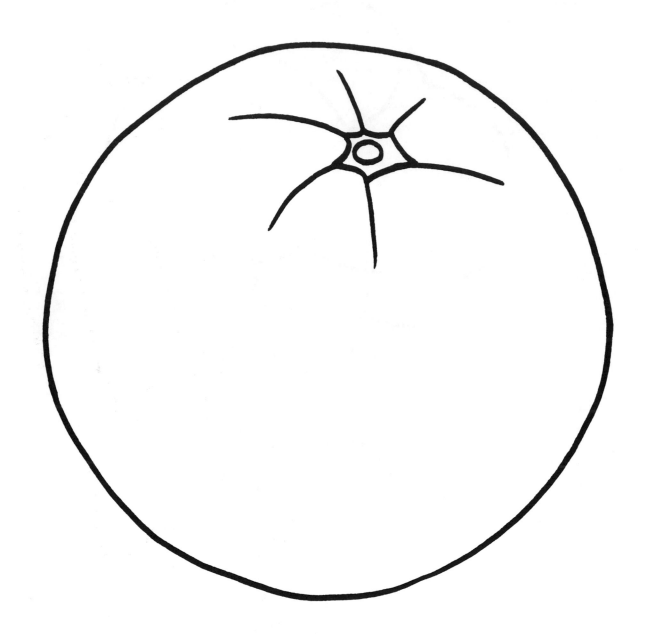

orange

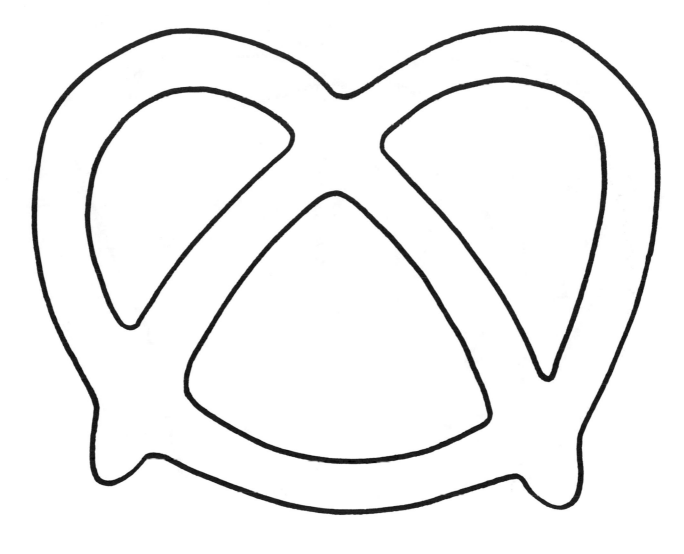

pretzel

strawberry

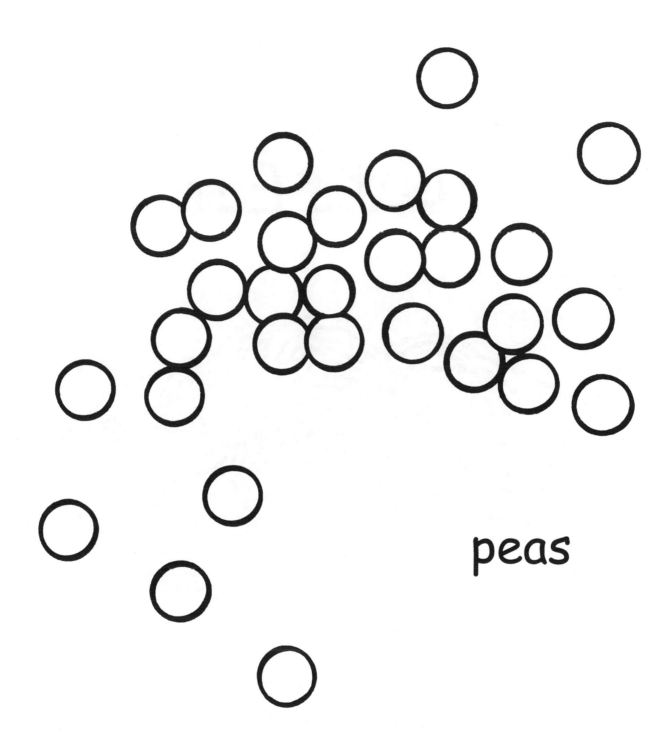

peas

# Let's Eat

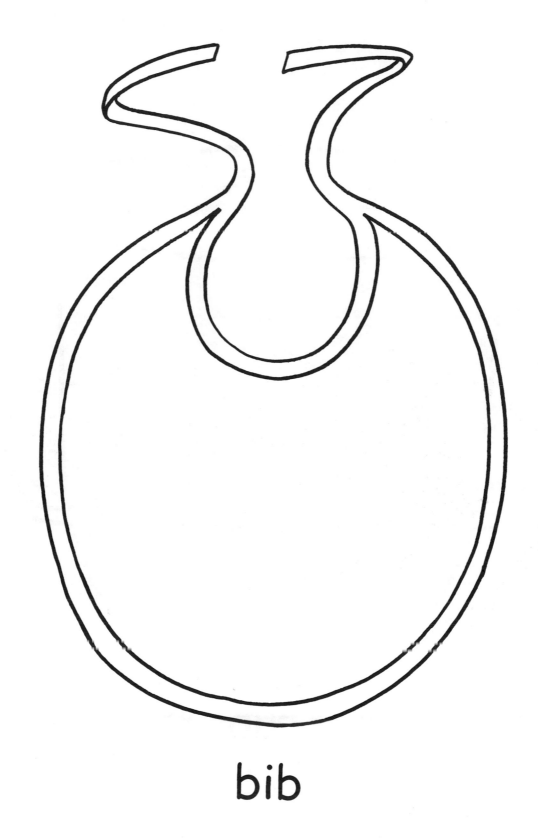

bib

cup

spoon

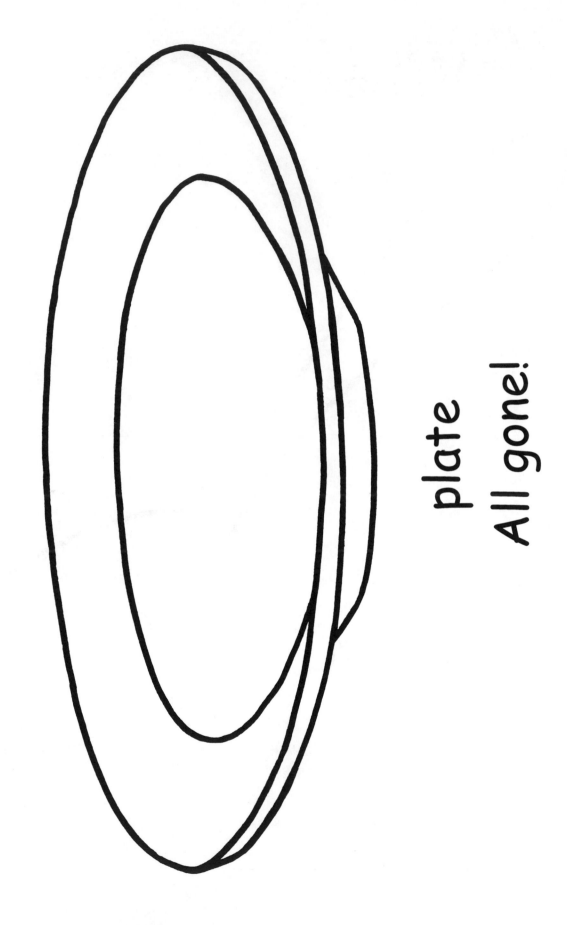

plate
All gone!

# Where Is Your Bellybutton?

This activity requires you to construct a large figure by combining the patterns on the following two pages. When presenting, point to the part of the body on the figure, name it, and ask the children to show you where it is on their bodies: "Here's the head. Where is your head?" Do the same for hair, eyes, nose, mouth, neck, arms, hands, fingers, bellybutton, legs, knees, feet, and toes.

# Let's Play

jack-in-the-box

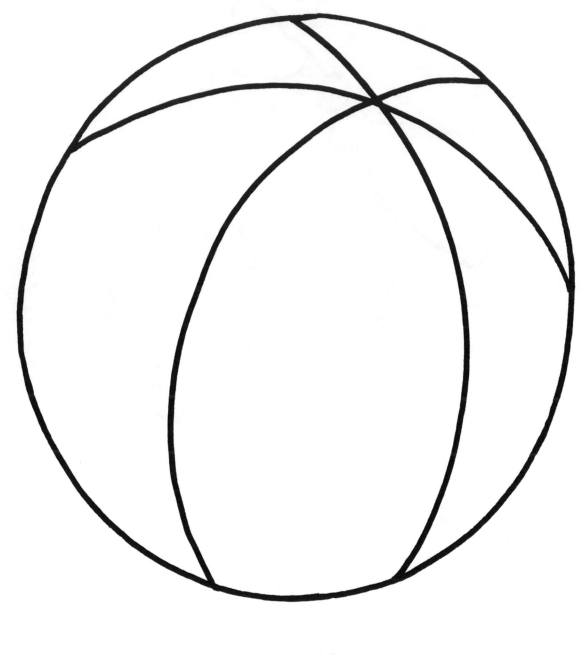

ball

bunny

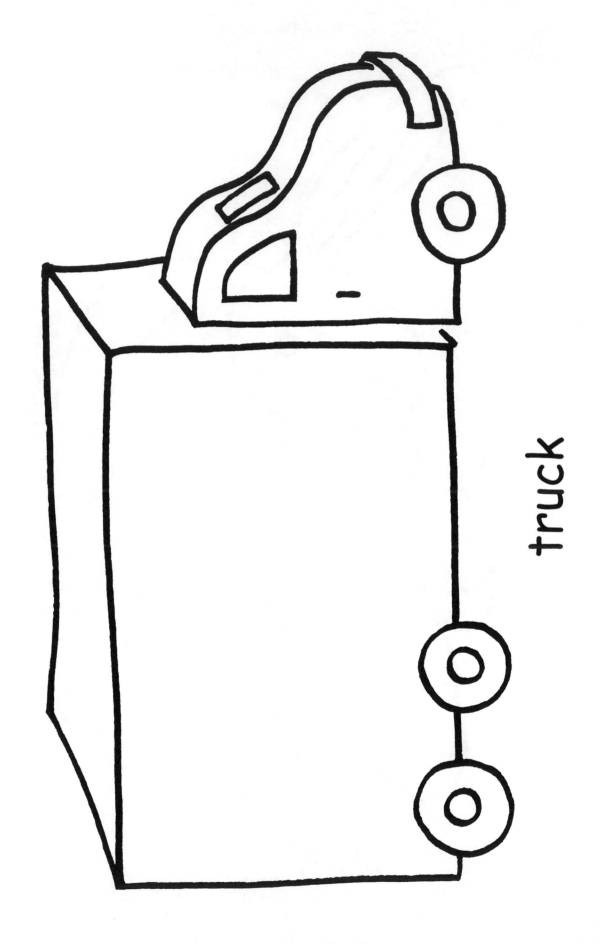

truck

82

keys

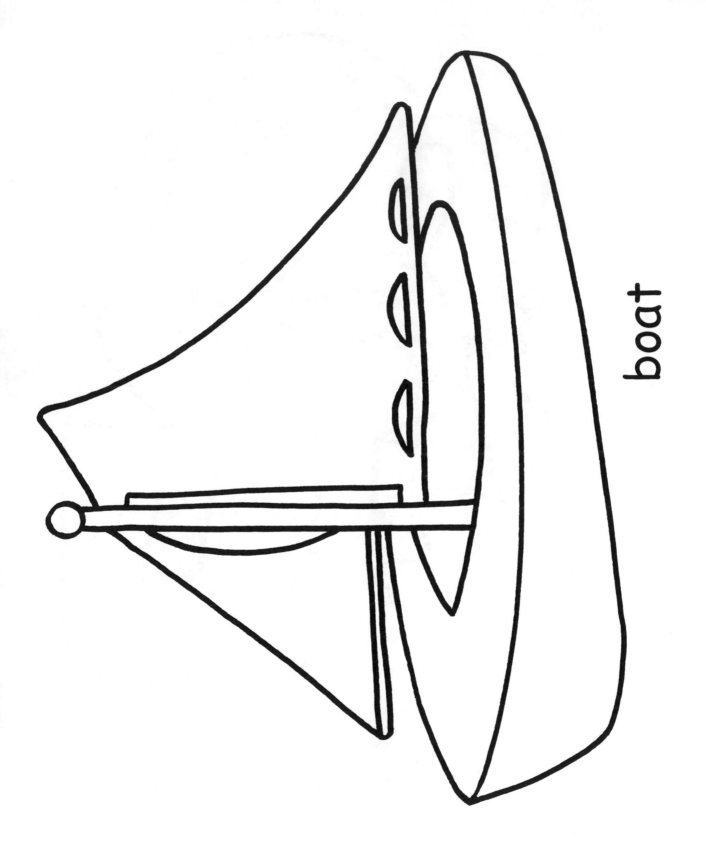

boat

84

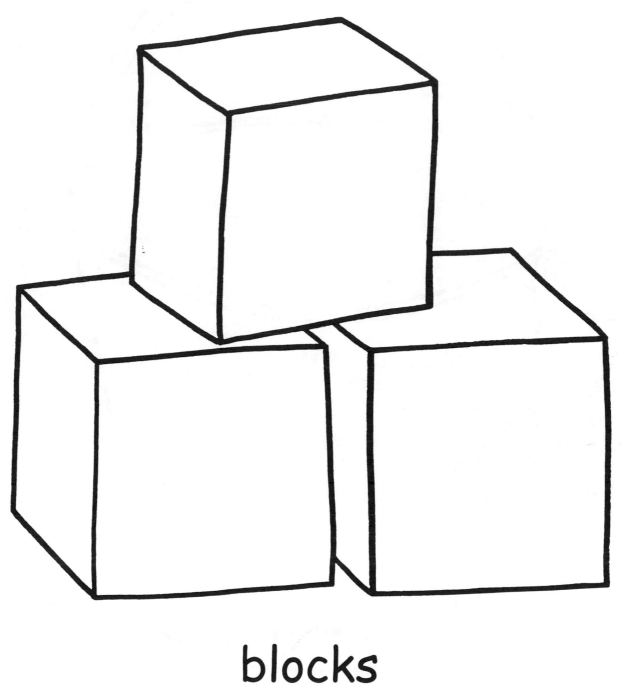

blocks

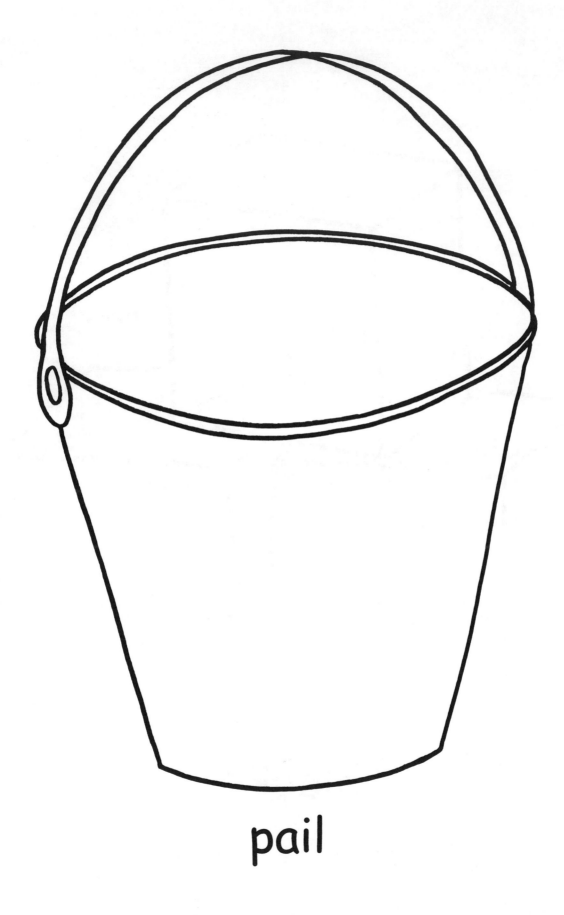

pail

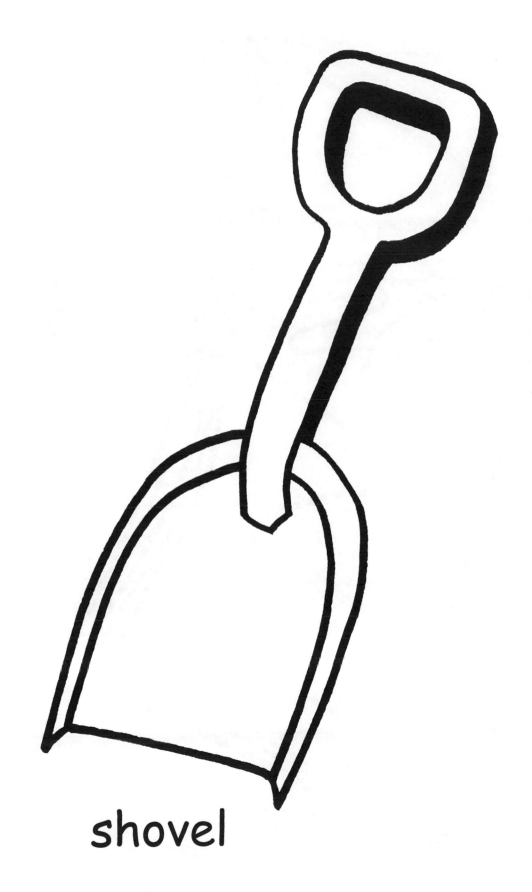

shovel

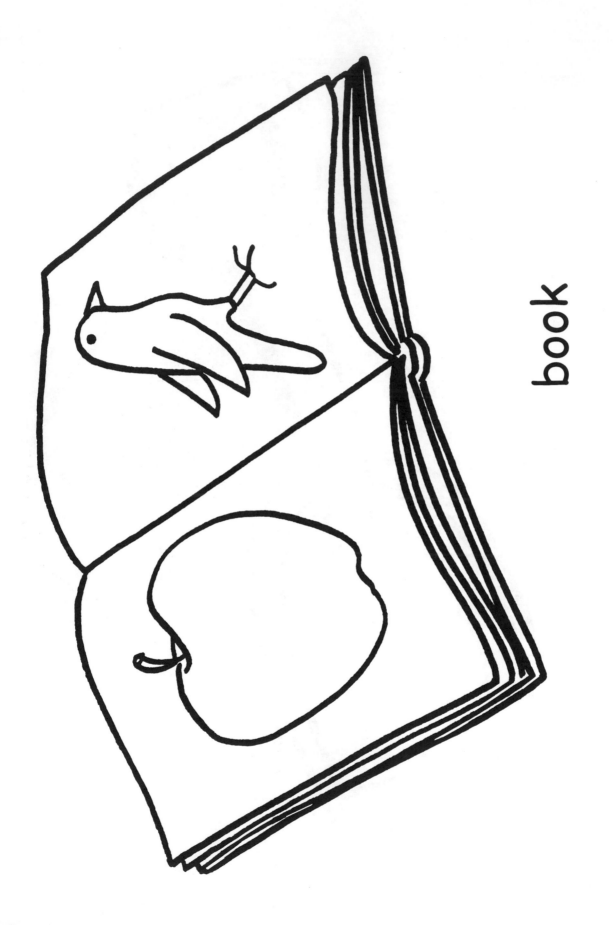

book

telephone

duck

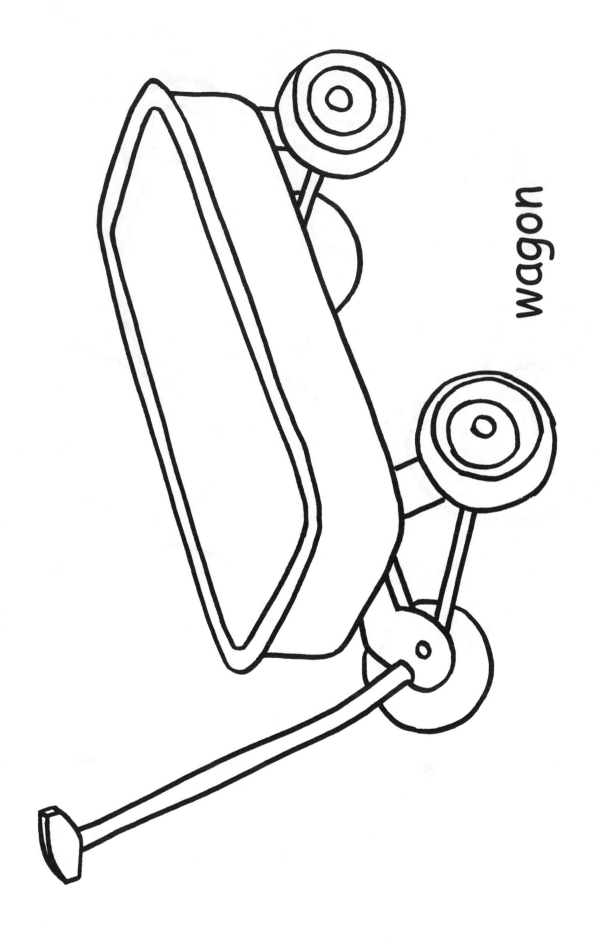

wagon

teddy bear

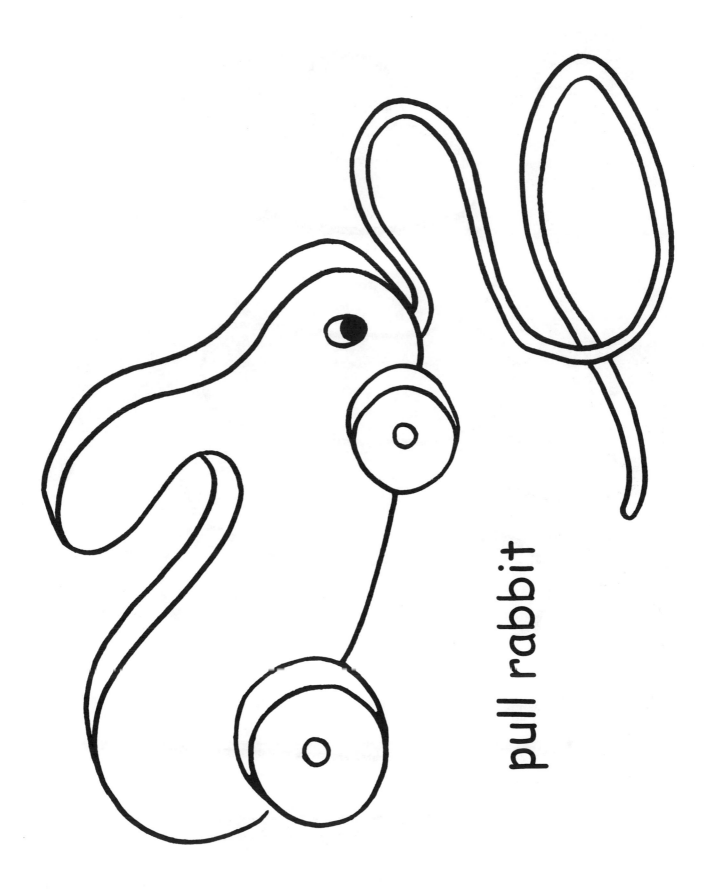

pull rabbit

stacking rings

Let's play!

# What Do You See Outside?

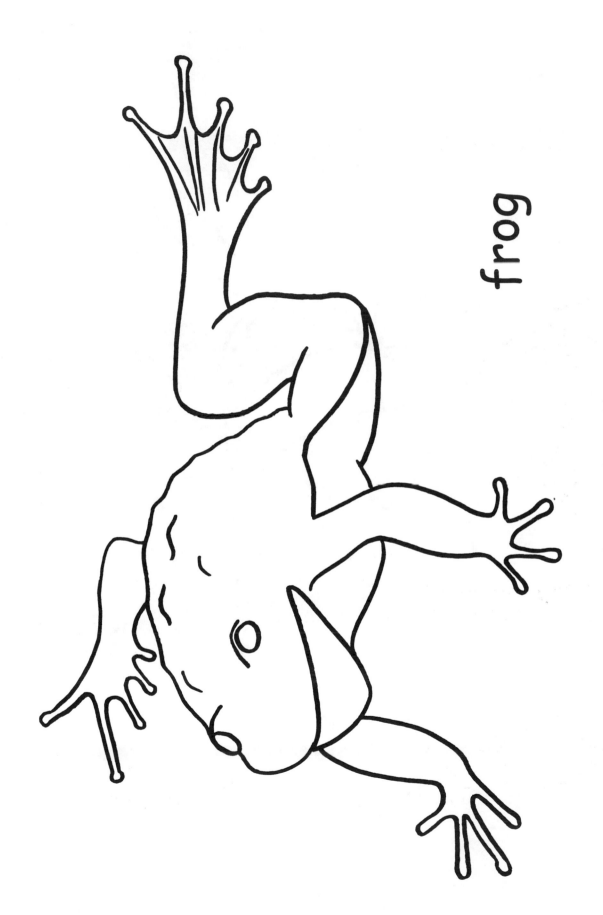

frog

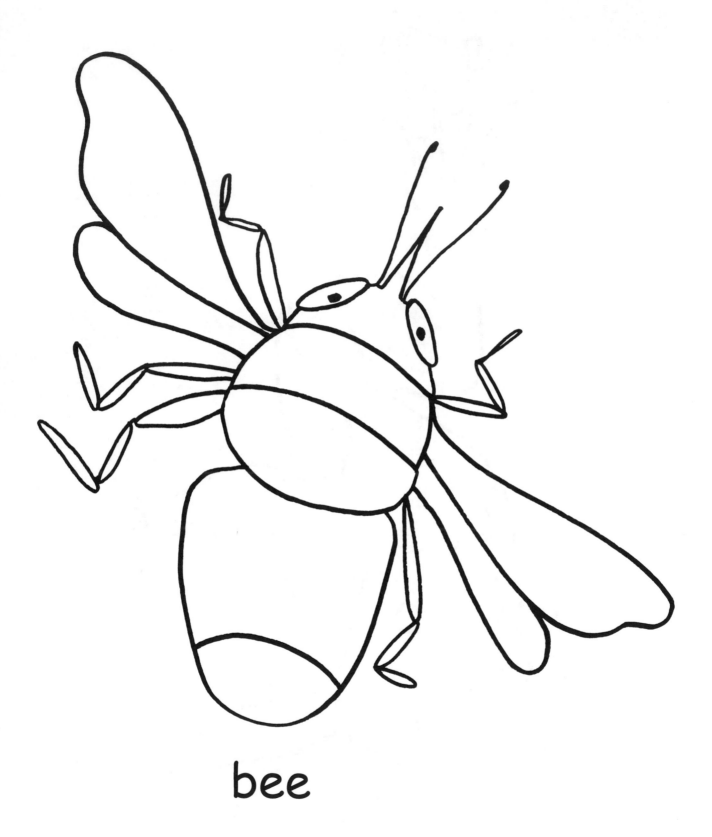

bee

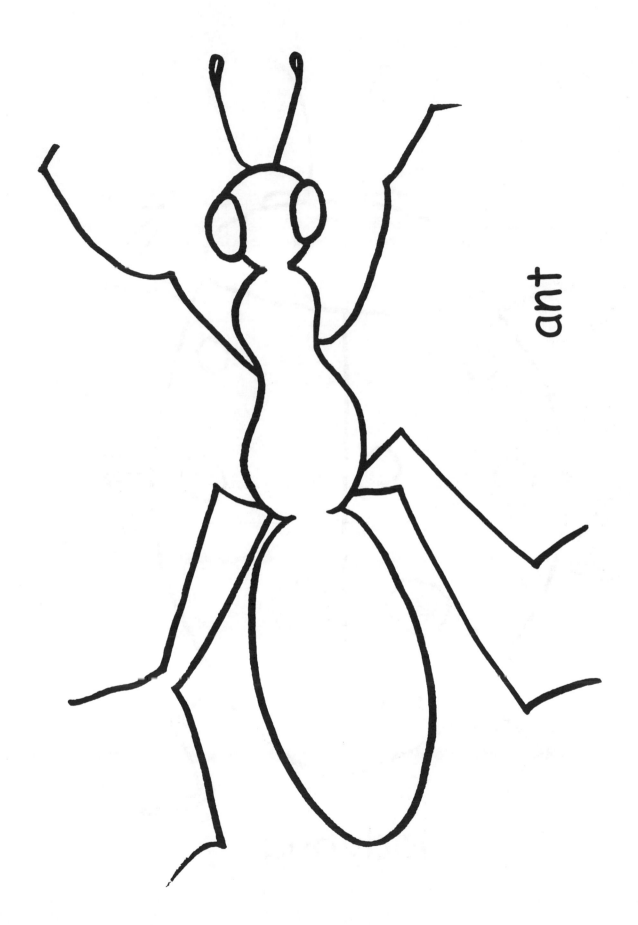

ant

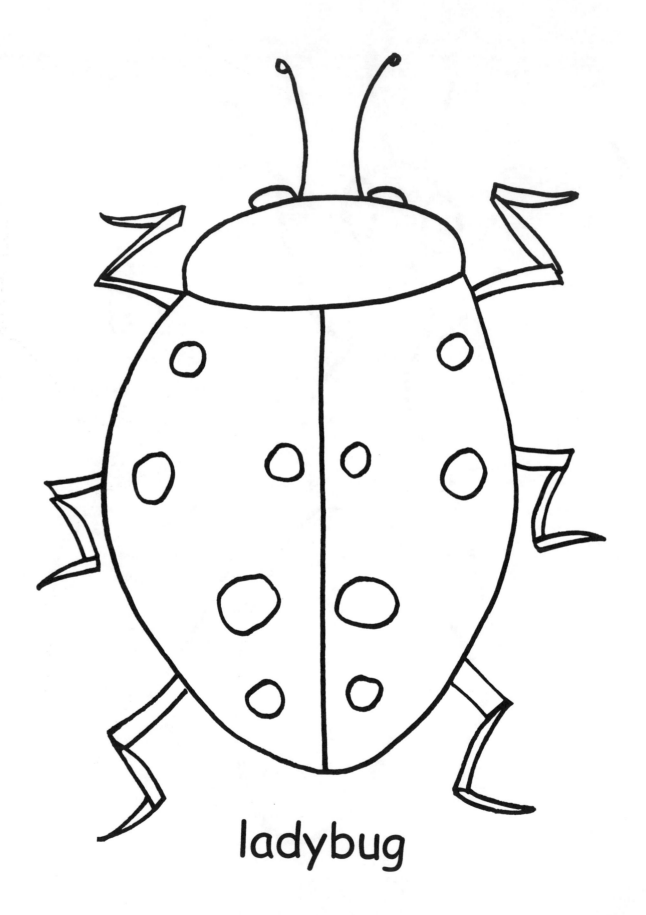

ladybug

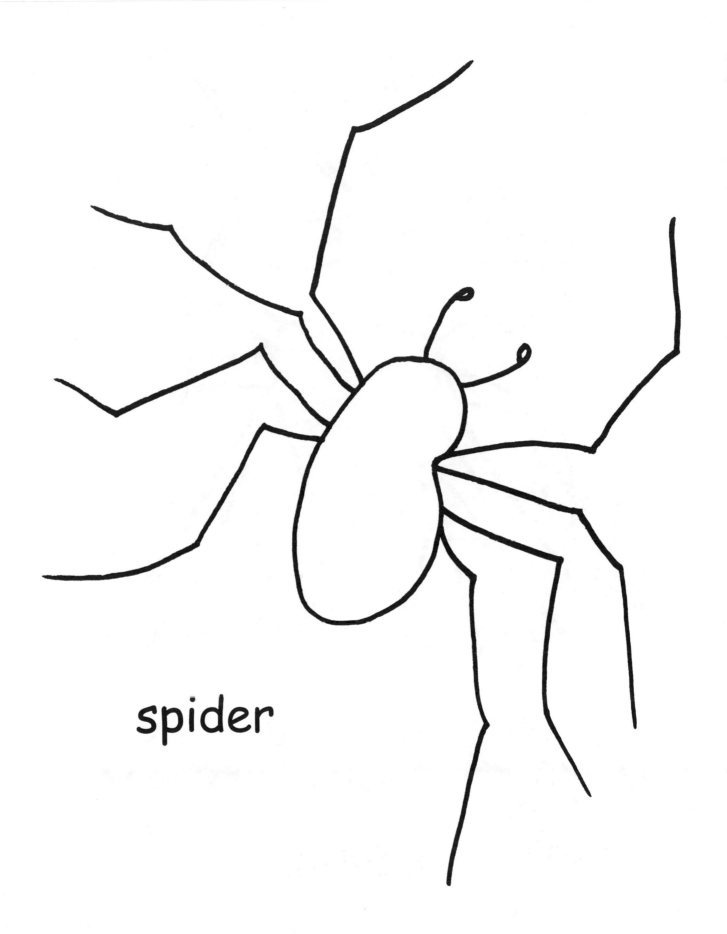

spider

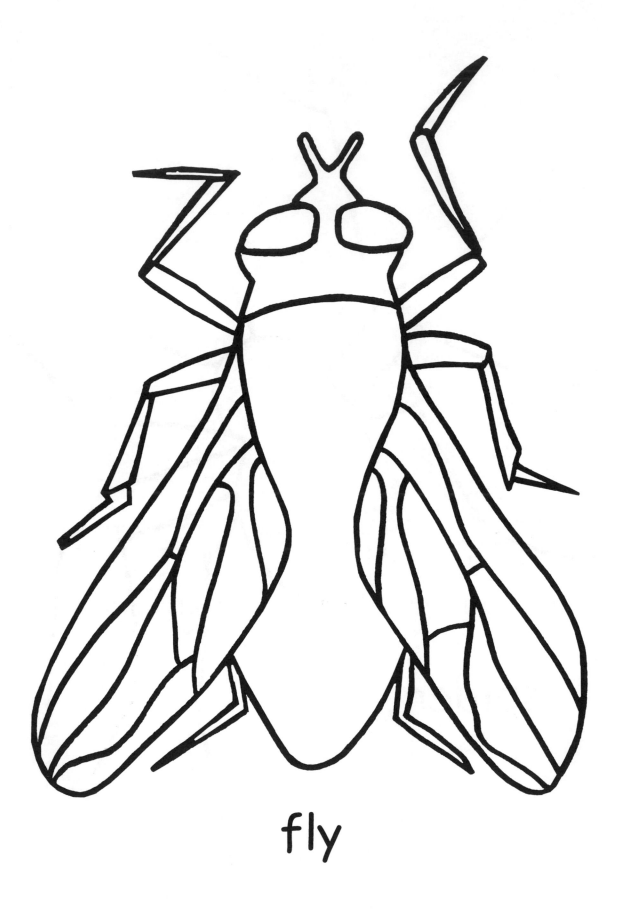

fly

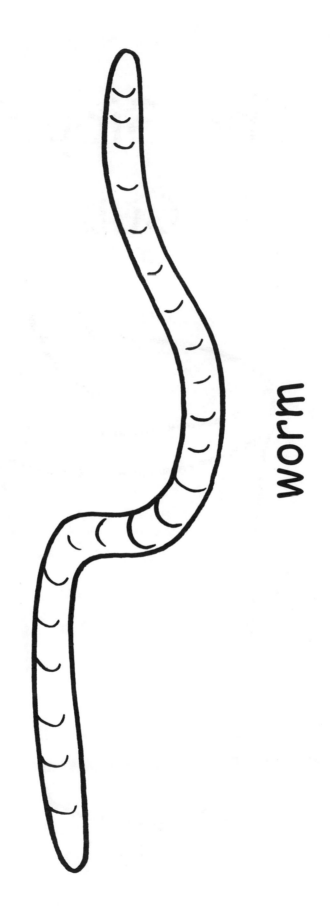

worm

# The Sipping Cup

I shake it,

Drip it,

And push it on the floor.

I sip and sip and sip it,

And then I say, "More."

# The Ball

I walk to the middle
of the room,

And I pick up my ball.

I put my feet apart firmly,
so I do not fall.

I roll the ball through,
using both my hands.

Then turn and run fast
to where it lands.

My legs are like a tunnel
when I play this game.

The ball going through the tunnel is a lot like a train.

# The Game

I will run, run, run away from you.

Chase me, Mommy, chase
me do!

I am laughing, laughing as I run from you.

Catch me, Mommy,

Catch me do!

# Pulling and Pushing

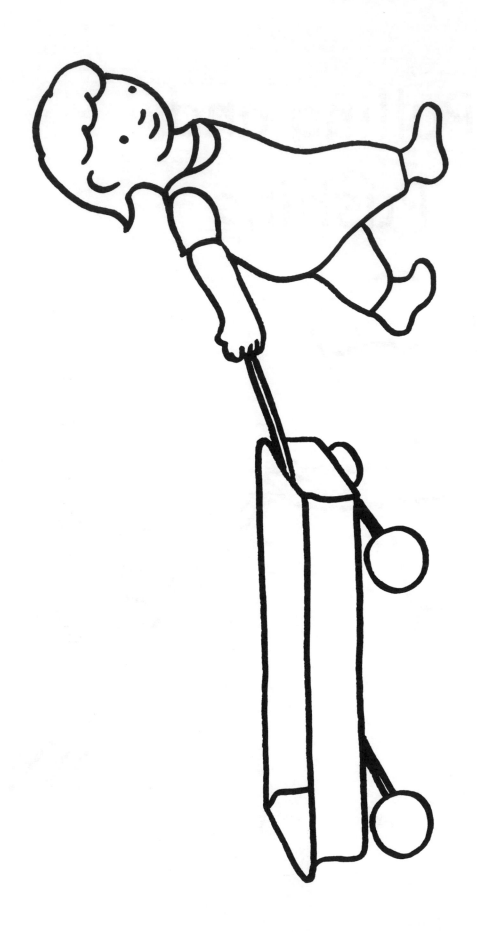

When I was little,
I liked to pull my wagon.

My wooden toy.

127

Even an old shopping bag.

Now I like to push.
I push my popper,

My shopping cart,

And my mop across
the floor.

I like to push and steer.
Soon I'll be able to drive!

# How Things Move

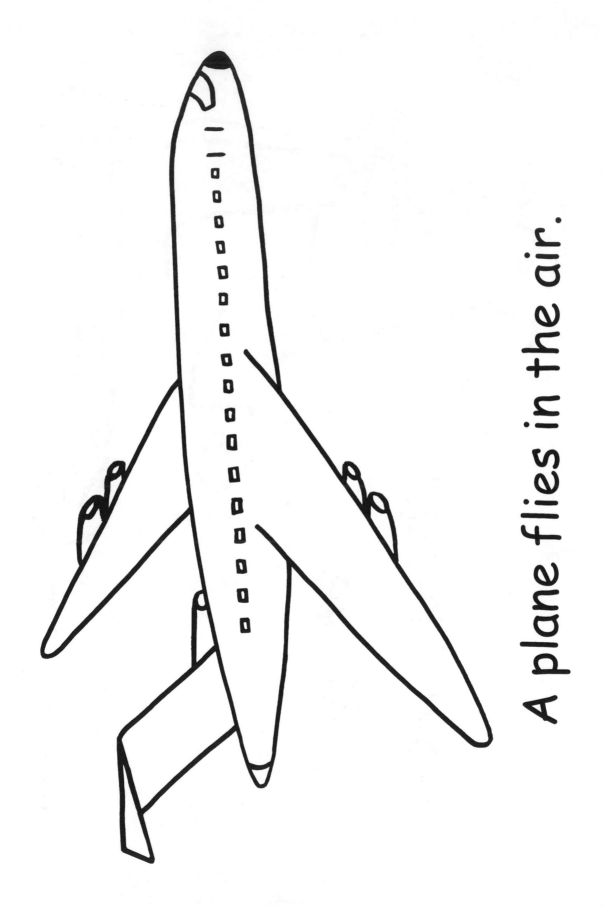

A plane flies in the air.

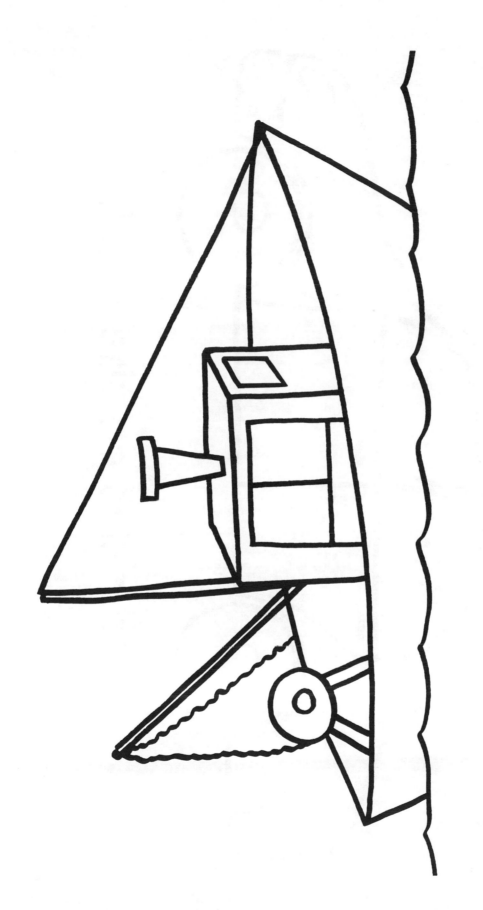

A boat floats on the water.

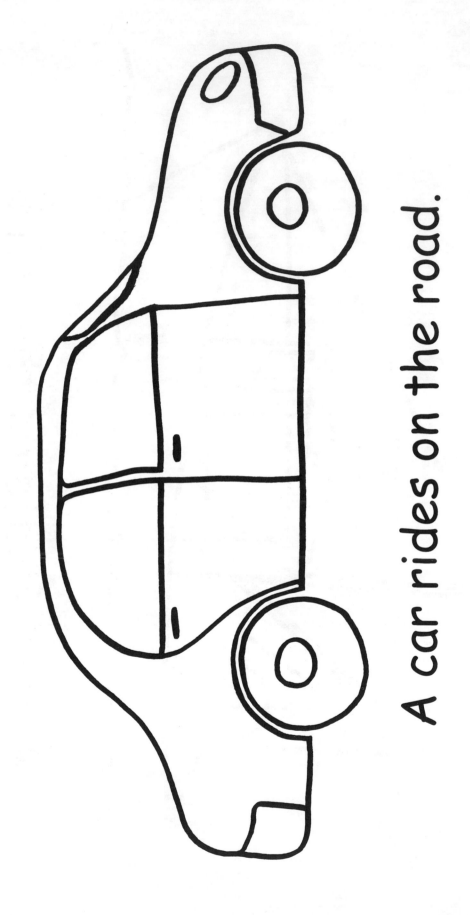

A car rides on the road.

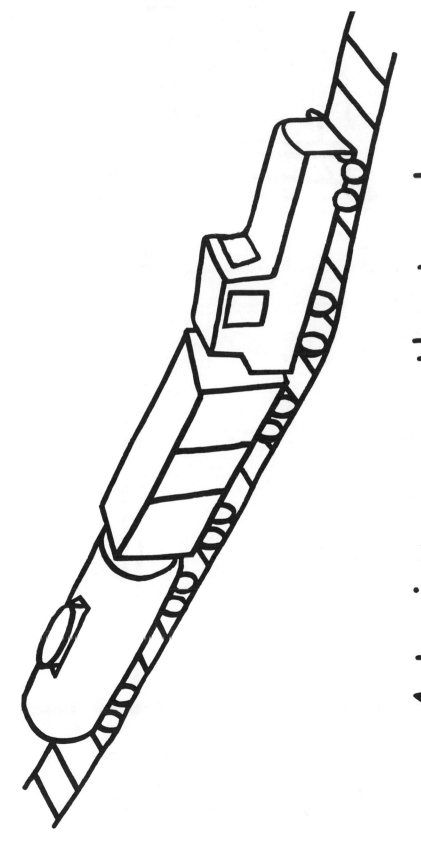

A train runs on the tracks.

A truck travels on the highway.

My dog and I walk on the ground.

139

# Flannelboard Patterns

## Traditional Chants and Nursery Rhymes

# Five
# Little
# Monkeys

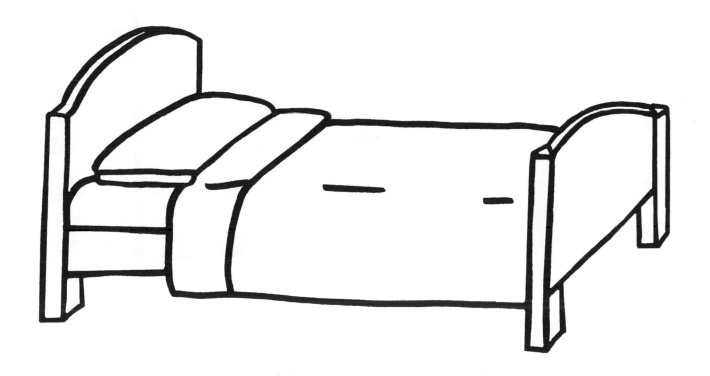

Keep the bed on the flannelboard while you place the monkeys above the bed.

144

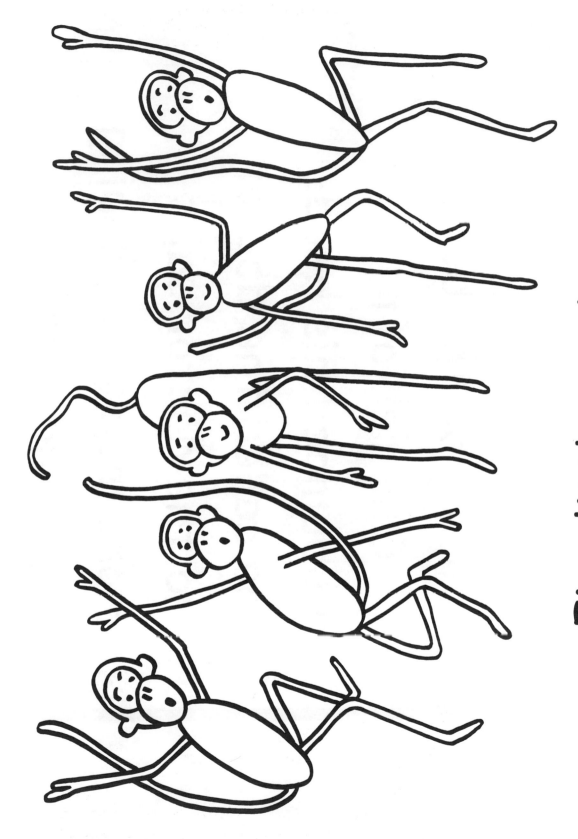

Five little monkeys

Repeat this refrain with four, three, two, and one monkey.

Jumping on the bed,

One fell off

And bumped his head.

Mama called the doctor

And the doctor said:

"No more monkeys jumping

on the bed!"

Four little monkeys

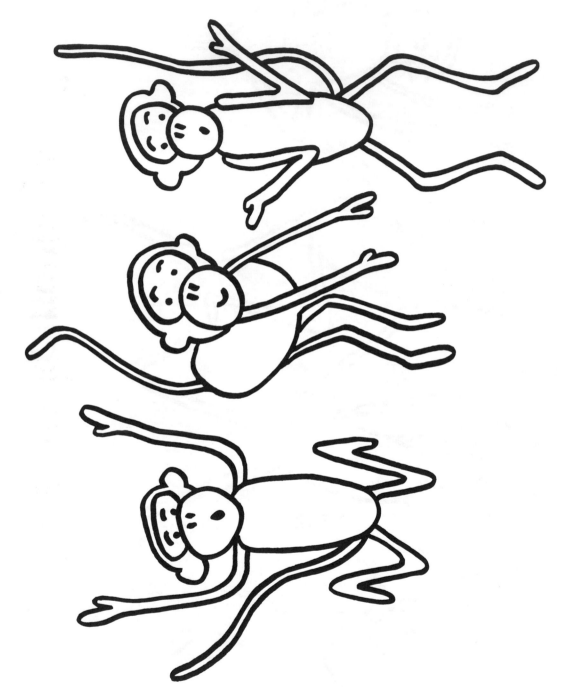

Three little monkeys

Two little monkeys

One little monkey

The wheels on the bus go round
and round, round and round,
round and round.

The wheels of the bus go
round and round,
All through the town.

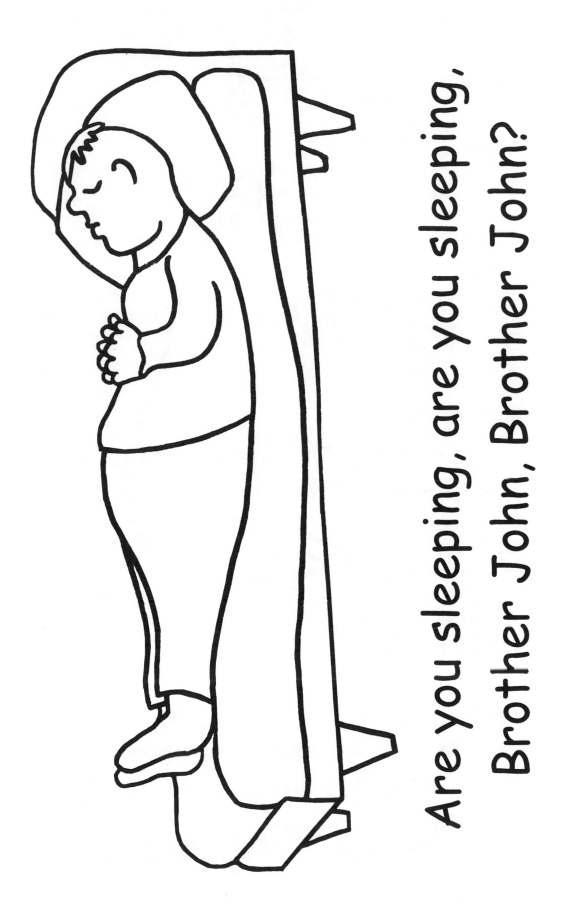

Are you sleeping, are you sleeping, Brother John, Brother John?

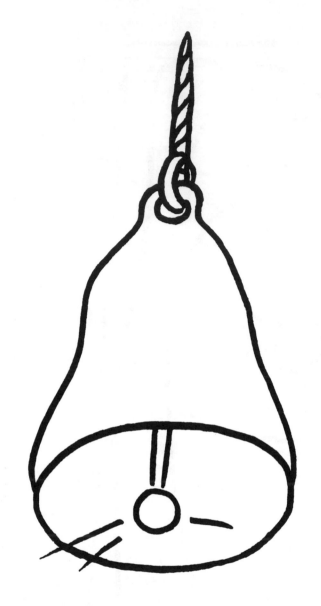

Morning bells are ringing,
Morning bells are ringing,
Ding, ding, dong,
Ding, ding, dong.

# Five Little Ducks

Place this figure on the right side of your board and leave it there during the entire poem. Place the pieces with the ducklings on the left side of the board.

# This is Mother duck.

Five little ducks went out one day,

Over the pond and far away.

Mother duck said,

"Quack, quack, quack, quack," ...

157

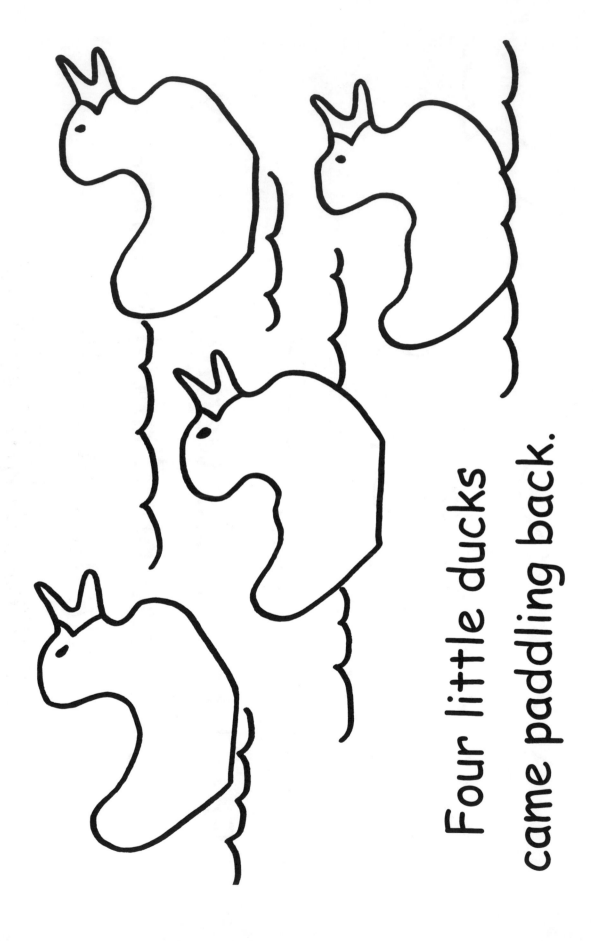

Four little ducks
came paddling back.

158

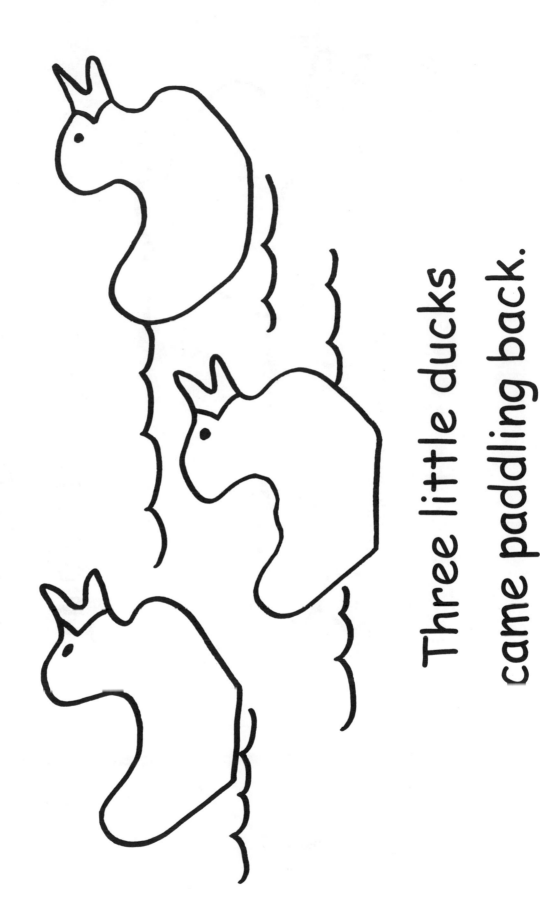

Repeat the initial verse with four, three, two, one, and no little ducks coming back.

# Three little ducks
# came paddling back.

Two little ducks
came paddling back.

One little duck
came paddling back.

No little ducks
came paddling back.

Then, Mother duck shouted,
"QUACK, QUACK, QUACK."

162

Five little ducks came paddling back.

I scream, you scream.

We all scream for ice cream.

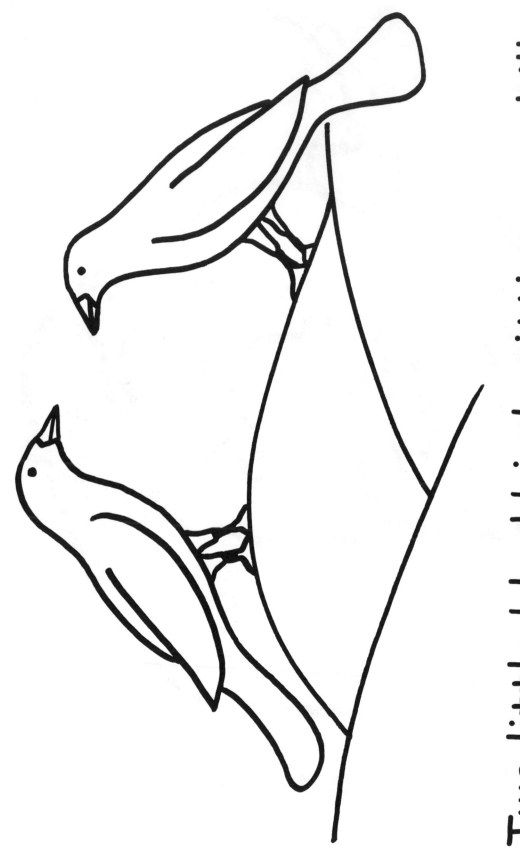

Two little blackbirds sitting on a hill,
One named Jack and one named Jill.

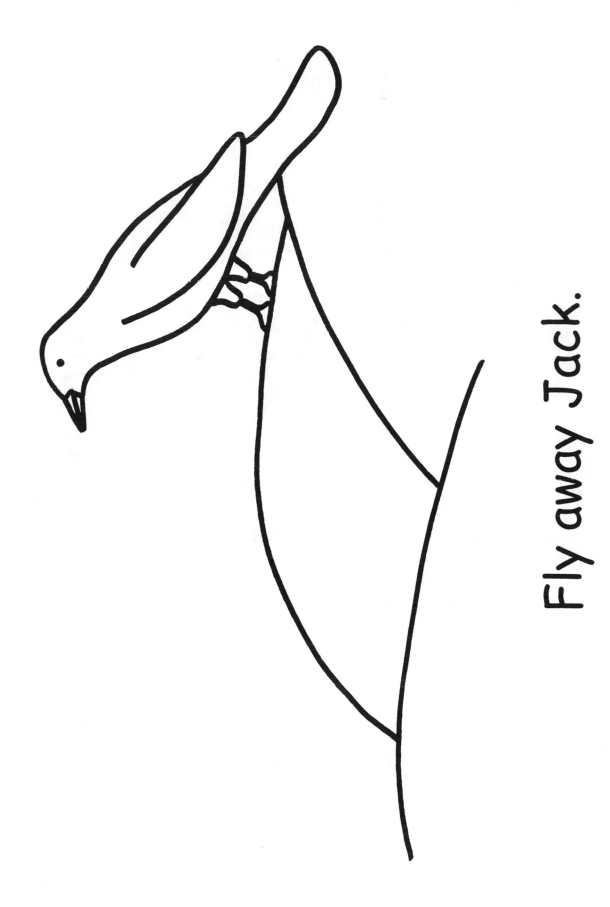

Fly away Jack.

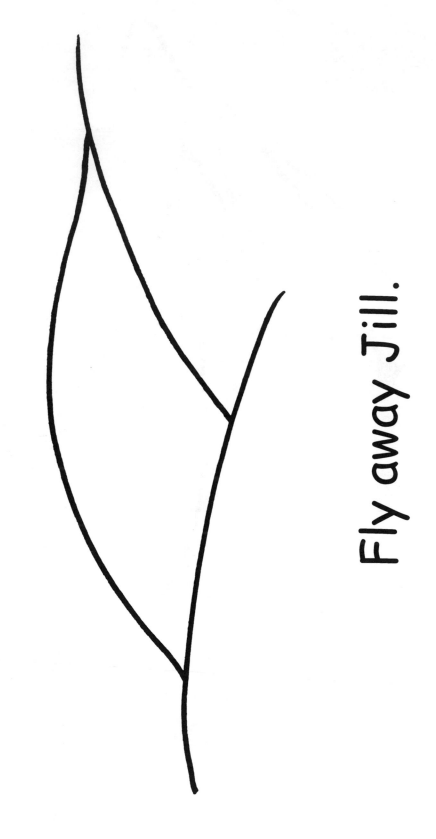

Fly away Jill.

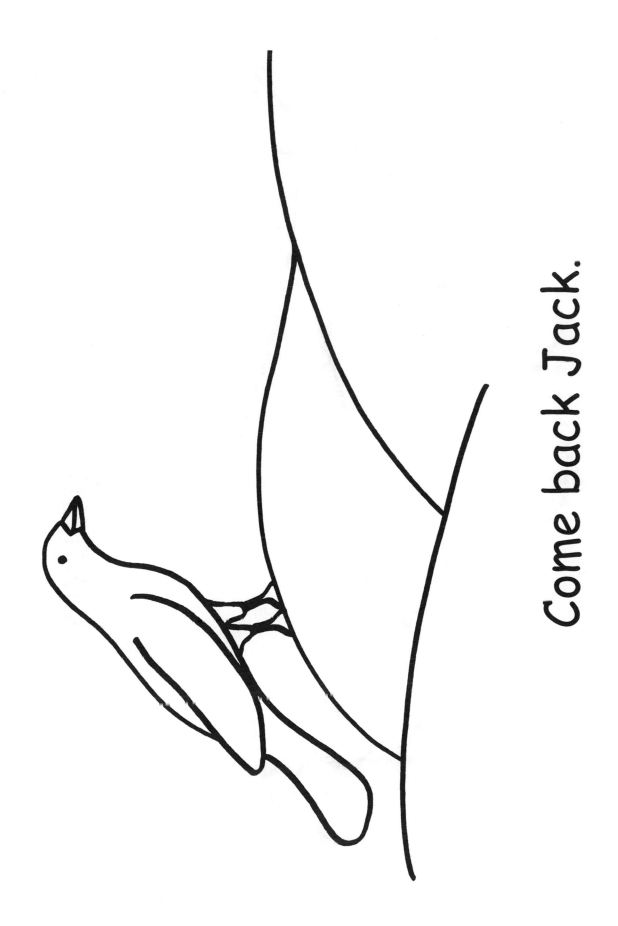

Come back Jack.

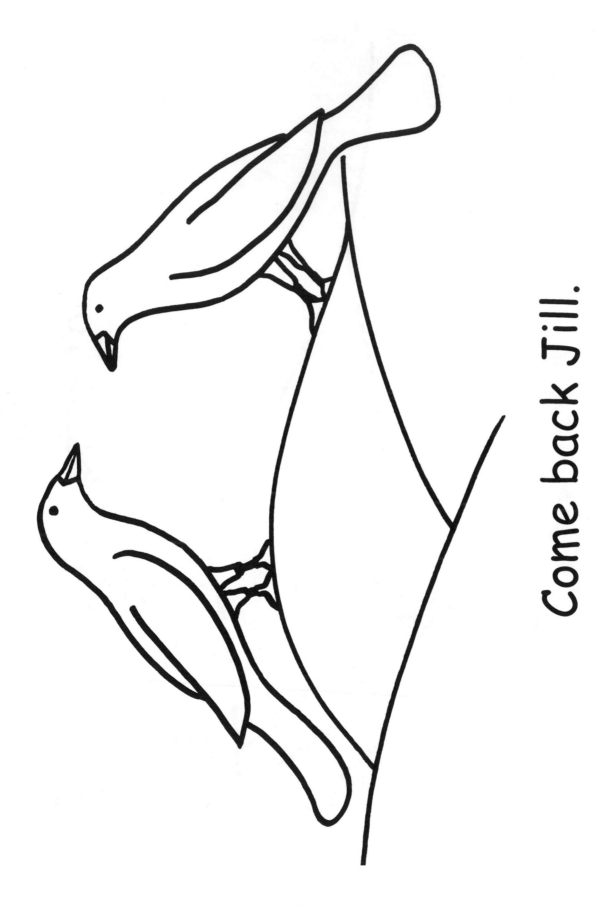

Come back Jill.

Two little blackbirds,
Sitting on a hill,
One named Jack,
And the other named Jill.

Bow wow wow wow,
Whose dog are thou?
Little Tom Tinker's dog,
Bow wow wow.

172

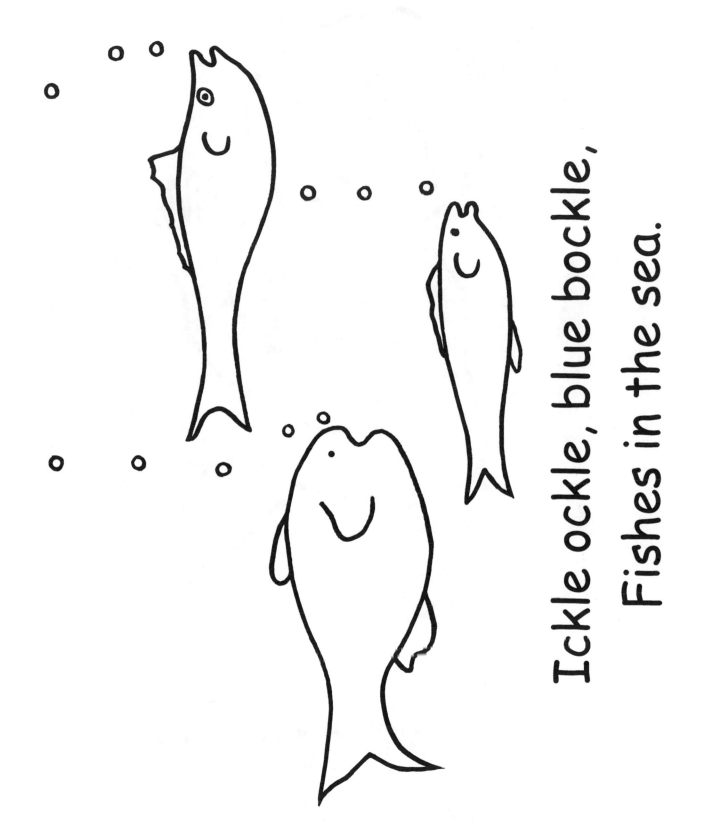

Ickle ockle, blue bockle,
Fishes in the sea.

If you want a fun baby,
please choose me.

Jack be nimble,
Jack be quick,
Jack jump over
the candlestick.

Where oh where has my
little dog gone?
Where oh where can he be?
With his tail so short and
his ears so long,
Where oh where can he be?

# Applety
# Pie

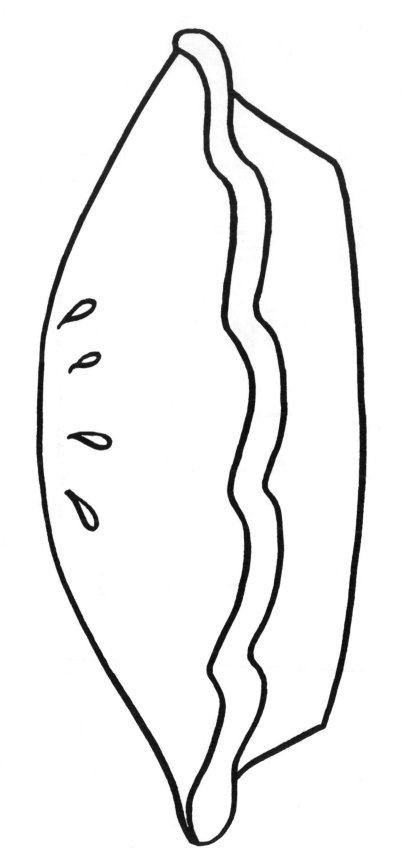

Round about, round about,
Applety pie.

178

My father loves pie and so do I.

Pat-a-cake, pat-a-cake,
Baker's man,

Bake me a cake
as fast as you can.
Pat it and prick it,
and mark it with a B,

Put it in the oven
for Baby and me.

Here am I, Little Jumping
Joan. When nobody's
with me, I'm all alone.

One, two, three, four, five,
Once I caught a fish alive.
Six, seven, eight, nine, ten,
Then I let it go again.
Why did you let it go?

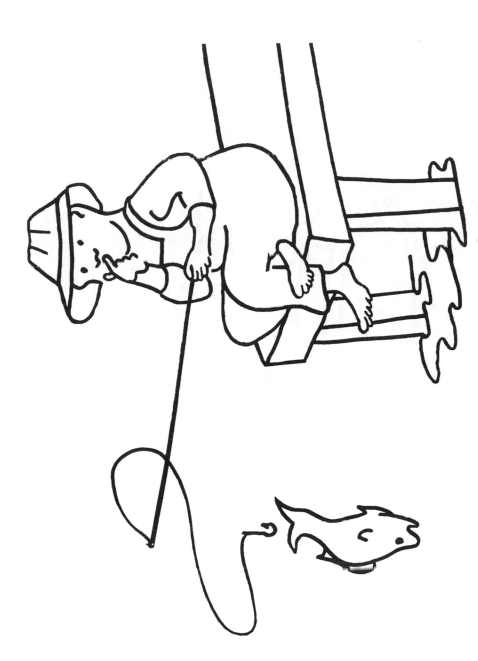

Because it bit my finger so.

Which finger did it bite?

This little finger on the right.

185

This little pig went
to market.

This little pig stayed home.

This little pig had bread and jam.

This little pig had none.

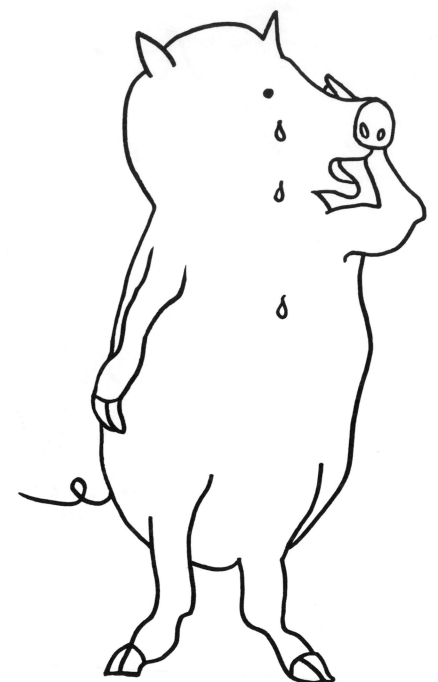

And this little pig cried
wee-wee-wee
all the way home.

Ring around the roses,
A pocketful of posies,

Ashes, ashes,
We all fall down.
Boom!

# Index

Ann D. Carlson conducted her first toddler storytime over twenty years ago as a children's librarian at the Orlando Public Library. Since then, her interests have centered on literature and library programs in early childhood. She is the author of *Early Childhood Literature Sharing Programs in Libraries* (Shoe String Press, 1985) and *The Preschooler & the Library* (Scarecrow Press, 1991). She has taught library services for children, children's literature, and early childhood development at the university level. Currently she is an Associate Professor at the Graduate School of Library and Information Science at Dominican University in River Forest, Illinois.

Mary Carlson has been an artist making sculpture for the past twenty-five years. Her work has been exhibited in numerous one-person and group shows in this country and in Europe. She has been the recipient of National Endowment for the Arts and John Simon Guggenheim fellowships. Currently she teaches art at Pratt Institute in Brooklyn. This is the first time she has illustrated a book. She lives in New York City most of the time.